Publish Your Book On Amazon

The Easy Way To Get In Print

by

Helen Stothard

First published 2012

www.hlspublishing.com

ISBN-13: 978-1479351220
ISBN-10: 1479351229

Copyright © Helen Stothard

All rights reserved. No part of this publication may be reproduced, stored or transmitted in any form, or by any means, electronic, mechanical or photocopying, recording or otherwise, without express written permission of the author.

Limit of Liability/Disclaimer of Warranty: This book is designed to provide information about the subject matter. It is sold with the understanding that the publisher and authors are not engaged in rendering legal, coaching or other professional services. While the publisher and author have used their best efforts in preparing this book, they make no representations or warranties with respect to the accuracy or completeness of the contents of this book and specifically disclaim any implied warranties of merchantability or fitness for a particular purpose. No warranty may be created or extended by sales representatives or written sales materials. This book is not intended or should be a substitute for therapy or professional advice. The views and opinions expressed in this page are strictly those of the author. The advice and strategies contained herein may not be suitable for your situation. The publisher is not engaged in rendering professional services, and you should consult a competent professional where appropriate. Neither the publisher nor author shall be liable for any loss of profit or any other commercial damages, including but not limited to special, incidental, consequential, or other damages. This document is provided for educational purposes only. The reader assumes all risk and responsibility for the usage of any information or ideas contained in this guide. If you do not wish to be bound by the above, you may return the book to the publisher for a full refund.

ACKNOWLEDGEMENTS

This book wouldn't have been possible if people hadn't believed in me and helped convince me to write my first book.

Others encouraged my love affair with publishing, entrusting me with their cherished manuscripts, and together we shared the dream that is seeing your published book land on your doorstep, freshly delivered by the postman. It truly is one of life's great and treasured moments.

I would therefore like to thank, in no particular order:

Sarah Bradley, Rachel Brett, Carole Meyrick, Nikki Pilkington, Heather Townsend, Gary Gorman, Geoff Ramm, Dean Mansell, Sigrid de Kaste, Jonathan Senior, Judith Morgan, Nicola G Marshall and Lucinda Latimer for their encouragement and faith. I am proud to have worked with you all.

I dedicate this book to my amazing mother, who encouraged my dream, and never once told me I couldn't reach the stars. I love you Mum xx

CONTENTS

Acknowledgements 3

Introduction 7

Praise for How to publish your book on Amazon 9

Praise for Helen Stothard's other books 10

Why should you publish in print? 12

What should you include in your book? 13

Research your book market 14

Make sure you deliver on your books promise 17

Review a book you've purchased 19

Revise your book 21

Format your book 22

Ask for reviews of your book 28

Layout: Title Page 29

Layout: Copyright Page 30

Layout: Dedication Page 31

Layout: Table of Contents 32

Layout: Reviews 34

Layout: Introduction 35

Layout: Content 36

Layout: Author Information 37

Write your book description 38

Book Cover 39

Proof Reading 44

Start thinking about pricing 46

Decide on your books category 50

Select your books key words 51

Write your Amazon Author Biography 53

Revise your book description... 54

Set up a landing page for your book 55

Proof Read, Proof Read and do it again............................... 56

Convert your manuscript to PDF.. 69

Sign up for your Createspace Publishing Account.................... 57

Enter your Royalty Information.. 60

Start your first project... 63

Set Up: Title Information 65

Set Up: ISBN.. 67

Set Up: Interior 69

Set Up: Automated Print Check... 75

Set Up: Cover.. 82

Set Up: Complete Setup 83

Set Up: Approve your Proof 85

Set Up: Sales Channels... 88

Set Up: Pricing 90

Set Up: Description 92

Set Up: Order your Book... 94

Your book is live 95

Sign up for your Amazon author page 96

Reporting.. 99

Amending your book or price.. 100

Don't Do It Yourself 101

About Helen Stothard 102

Contact Helen Stothard 104

INTRODUCTION

Welcome to 'Publish your book on Amazon: the easy way to get in print'.

Have you always wanted to be an author and see your name on a book cover? Well now you can. With this book I will help you take your existing eBook, manuscript or Kindle book and publish it yourself on Amazon.

This book will show you:

- How to set up your Createspace account

- Tips and tricks on how to format your book so that it looks right in print

- How to price and market your book

- How to set up your Amazon Author page

- What you should include in your book

- How to ensure your book is found on Amazon and more!

I am an established Kindle and print publisher and author, and will use my experience to make this journey as easy and stress free as possible for you.

And from experience I can tell you there is no feeling like logging onto Amazon and seeing your book on there!

Helen

PRAISE FOR HOW TO PUBLISH YOUR BOOK ON AMAZON

" I found this a very easy read, free of the unnecessary proliferation often found in self help and guidance books. I thought the layout was spot on, again making the book easy to follow and it scanned well

The introduction was brief, to the point and delivered on what to expect from the book. I think in general for people like myself looking to self publish it will work well as support literature when working my way through the Createspace experience which at first glance appears quite daunting!"

Richard Ogando

PRAISE FOR HELEN STOTHARD'S OTHER BOOKS

The A to Z of Small Business Tools

"From the opening chapter the author Helen Stothard takes you by the hand and skilfully guides you through the maze that is the electronic app world, at every step describing and explaining their use, especially from the small business persons perspective.

Helen, owner of HLSBS.com clearly understands the requirements of today's modern small business, and although offers simple and clear advice, also discusses quite complex and advanced strategies, perfect for both first time business start up or seasoned serial entrepreneur.

Having been a business owner myself for 10 years, I was quite happy to believe that this dog had seen most of the tricks of the trade, yet Helen managed to bring me bang up to date in many areas, and has proved my offices business communications systems efficiency, hopefully saving my organisation valuable time, whilst allowing it to appear to offer better customer services to clients.

I would highly recommend this book to not just the small business owner, but I would also encourage any business executive, or mumpreneur or blogger to reach to the virtual book shelf and pull down a copy of this business persons Bible of how to !"

How to get started on Twitter and Generate Business

"I would highly recommend this book to anyone who uses or wants to use Twitter.

It is easy to read, explains things in simple terms and gives you instructions on how to get going so you are up and running in minutes.

Can be read in 30 minutes and you can apply what you read only seconds later"

WHY SHOULD YOU PUBLISH IN PRINT?

Quite simply because you will boost your online exposure and revenue.

Whilst you may have read that the Kindle is the rising star in publishing you have to remember that not everyone has one yet, nor wants one. By restricting yourself to only one medium you are lowering the potential market for your book.

You may have a PDF or Kindle book already. Making your book available in print broadens your audience.

Once you've done the hard part and published your book in print it's a case of sitting back and reaping the benefits. Okay you will have to promote your book, but, once the initial work is done Createspace pay your commission direct to your bank account for you every month. What could be simpler.

WHAT SHOULD YOU INCLUDE IN YOUR BOOK?

The hardest part of writing a book is deciding on the book content. After all, the end result will hopefully be that people buy your book, so the content has to be something that they want or need.

You need to write and review your book plan. Write down the chapter headings and list what you need to include in each chapter. Layout this plan on paper.

Look at your plan – will this satisfy the reader? Will it deliver what you have promised?

Now look at your existing manuscript and ask yourself if what you have already written matches the book plan?

Does your book need revising to match the plan that you have written?

RESEARCH YOUR BOOK MARKET

Now we have planned our book we need to make sure that there is a market out there for it.

Ask yourself who is your target reader? Write your book for them.

Self published author John Locke has sold over a million books on Kindle, he was the 8th person to do that but the first self publishing author to achieve that status. Not bad without the support of a huge publishing house is it! His advice was to choose your niche and write for them.

If you write for too general an audience you end up pleasing no one.

Identify your niche market, find out what they want, what they like and what they need and incorporate that into your book.

Stay true to that and you will find that they will remain loyal to you as an author and promote your work for you as well.

I often speak to authors who want to publish one book that covers everything they know. However, this can be too generic for your audience, and as mentioned previously, you end up pleasing no one.

Look at what you already have in your manuscript. If it's a business book are there varying levels of information in there? If you have beginner, intermediate and advanced you may be better writing three separate books, one for each market.

Beginners will buy book one and want to progress, and you already have the material there for the next two levels.

Intermediate will buy the second book and then want to progress onto book three.

Advanced won't be interested in wasting time reading what they already know, they won't buy a book aimed at the novice, they want something that talks to them and will buy book three.

Can you see how one book wouldn't appeal to anyone but the beginner? Yet by spreading the content out you now appeal to all three markets?

Read through your manuscript again. Is it niche enough to attract a loyal audience, or is it so generic that anyone could pick it up, perhaps enjoy it, but not be enthralled enough by it to want to buy the next book in the series?

Of course if you only ever plan to write the one book that's fine, but do think ahead if possible. What if you do manage to hit that niche spot and your readers clamour for more? Can you accommodate them?

MAKE SURE YOU DELIVER ON YOUR BOOKS PROMISE

Whilst we touched on this in the previous chapter it needs looking at in more depth.

It might seem obvious but if people are going to buy your book you need to ensure that they will be receiving 'bang for their buck' or 'value for money'.

If we want positive reviews on Amazon (we'll cover this more later), we need to provide great content.

Have you ever bought a book only to be disappointed that it didn't meet your expectations? You bought it because it promised you x,y,z and yet it never delivered on the promise? It's a huge let down and we don't want that to happen with your book.

Ask yourself if your book will add value. What questions do you promise to answer for your reader and have you answered them?

Have you promised your reader a particular story line? Will your reader come away from your book feeling they got value for money or feeling let down?

Go back to the plan you wrote earlier and read through it, revise it if necessary to ensure you are meeting your readers expectations.

REVIEW A BOOK YOU'VE PURCHASED

I am sure like me you have books that you have read and loved, it would be useful for you to review that book on Amazon so you can understand the process your reader goes through.

Ask yourself:

- What did I like about the layout

- What didn't I like about the layout

- Did you notice typos?

- Did the author introduce you to the book, was it too short/too long?

- When you finished the book was there additional information there that was of value?

- Did the book live up to the description?

- If you paid full price for the book was it value for money?

- What would I have done differently?

- What aspects of the book worked really well and would translate to my book?

- Would I want to read more of this authors work and why? How could I use that to make my own book better?

Once you have considered all this, then log into Amazon and leave a review for the author, you may even want to click the 'like' button under the book title as this will also help their book reach a higher ranking.

If you're going to ask other people to review your book it's important that you understand the process that they go through.

REVISE YOUR BOOK

You've written your book plan and now we need to look at what you have already written and revise it to match your book plan and the improvements/edits you have decided to incorporate as a result of reading and reviewing someone else's book.

Read through your manuscript again. Does it still hold true to your original plan?

I don't know about you but every time I read one of my own books I want to tweak it, I think of something else to add, or a different way of phrasing a comment.

You could go on like this forever, however, set yourself a deadline and stick to it, but do at least one revision from the original manuscript.

FORMAT YOUR BOOK

There are lots of fancy tools out there to help you create your book but the simplest by far is Word, and that's how the whole process should be - simple!

Page Size
Your page size is critical and it must match the print size for your book. You can create a custom page size in Word using the page layout tab. Just select custom size under size and enter the relevant sizes. Createspace allows you to print to industry standard sizes or custom sizes but you need to consider again the reader experience and the cost of the various options.

My readers prefer a 5"x8" book as this fits in the bookcase, is the same as most fiction books and is small enough to fit into a handbag, although my business books were originally printed in A4. Some clients choose 6"x9" format in order to keep the number of pages down.

It's important to make this decision at the outset as it can take an awful lot of formatting and time to convert a manuscript from one size to another, although this is something I've got down pretty well now!

Interior - Colour or Black and White?
You may not think this is important but again it has to be decided before you submit your interior file. The big difference between the two is cost. It costs approximately three times as much to print a colour interior as a black and white one.

This means you either have to charge a very high selling price to make any royalty from the book, or you have to consider whether the images and colours need to be colour in the first place. Would black and white work just as well and help keep the print cost, and therefore the retail price, lower?

You can still work with colour in your manuscript and have colour in your interior file, just note that if you choose black and white interior then any instances of colour will be printed in varying shades of greyscale.

Font
Choose a font that is going to be easy to read in print. I like to use Arial as it looks good on the page but you can use other fonts if you prefer.

Chapters
In order to create a table of contents at the beginning of the book you will need to specify each chapter heading as a 'heading' in Word.

You may however want a more visual chapter heading but remember if it's not in text and specified as a heading your contents table will fail and you will have to manually create one. This can be extremely time consuming. If you are going to use images as chapter headings make sure you follow the rules below under images.

You can however increase the size of the chapter heading and play with the alignment and spacing to get it to stand out.

I have one client who wants each chapter to start on the right hand side of the book so this meant having to insert blank pages every so often if it didn't occur naturally.

Images
These should be added using the File – Insert – Picture option and not copied and pasted or they won't show up properly. It's a good idea to keep your images in a separate folder so that they are easy to find if you need to replace them later. If you can then number them in the order that they appear in the book, if you do need to edit a book later it's much easier if your images are in order. The most important thing to note is that your images need to be 300Dpi resolution so they work in print, anything less and they can appear pixellated.

If you haven't got a high enough resolution image then take a look at a free tool called Irfan View which allows you to resize the image and increase the dpi as well.

Paragraphs
I prefer to read a book that has justified text, but it's up to you how you lay your text out. If you want to appeal to the widest possible audience spend some time thinking about how easy your book is to read. If your font is small and your text is close together it could spoil your book for a reader who struggles to see it. Use a sensible sized font and 1.5 line spacing.
Don't have paragraphs that go on for the whole page, remember your reader needs to take a breath occasionally! I've seen some authors write paragraphs that take up a page and a half. It's not just about the story or the content, how it looks to the reader is important as well.

Header and Footer
Unlike Kindle you can have a header and footer in your print project. At the very least you should have a page number on each page.

Word allows you to have different headers and footers depending on whether the page is odd or even but one word of warning. When you add your book interior to Createspace it adds an extra page at the front. If you want your headers and footers to look right you have to do them the wrong way round in your manuscript. That means if you want the header to be left aligned on your left hand page and right aligned on your right hand page you set them up the other way round in your manuscript. This can take a little getting used to and if you're not comfortable with it just ensure your header and footer are centred.

I also use a dark grey text and smaller font for headers and footers as I don't want them to stand out more than the content.

Cover Image
You don't need to include the cover image in the main document as you load the cover image separately to the books interior.

Pages
Unlike Kindle you do have to consider the look of the page in your book interior. It will print exactly as it shows on your screen, so if you don't want a single line of text at the top of one page you need to consider revising the preceding text to prevent this, perhaps inserting a manual page break at the beginning of the sentence.

When you review your book interior later one of the things you need to check is that the top line of text on each page is lined up at the top of the page on the interior.

If you edit your manuscript it may change where the page breaks fall and sometimes a paragraph starts a line below the top of the page.

ASK FOR REVIEWS OF YOUR BOOK

You've nearly completed your manuscript and now would be a good time to send a sample copy to select members of your target audience and ask for their feedback and a review.

You'll be able to include some of these in your book description and in the front of the book before you publish, as well as when marketing the book via your website or newsletter.

LAYOUT:
TITLE PAGE

The first page in your manuscript should be a title page.

This only needs to be the book title with the author name underneath.

Of course, being me, I sometimes cheat and incorporate the title page and the copyright page as one, but let's set you off on the right path and have two separate pages!

LAYOUT:
COPYRIGHT PAGE

After your title page you need to insert a copyright page. According to Createspace templates all you need to show here is:

> Copyright © 2012 Author Name
> All rights reserved.
> ISBN:
> ISBN-13:

You will receive the ISBN numbers when you start creating the project on Createspace so you need to remember to come back and insert them later.

LAYOUT: DEDICATION PAGE

If you're going to include one then this is the third page in your manuscript, you may choose to have acknowledgements instead or combine the two.

The dedication page is followed by a blank page.

LAYOUT: TABLE OF CONTENTS

If you're going to have one this follows the blank page after the dedication page.

Unlike Kindle, page numbers do apply in your print book. Depending on the type of book you are writing you may want to include a table of contents to make it easier for your reader to navigate.

Go to the point in your document where you would like your Table of Contents to appear.
Click on References in your Word menu.

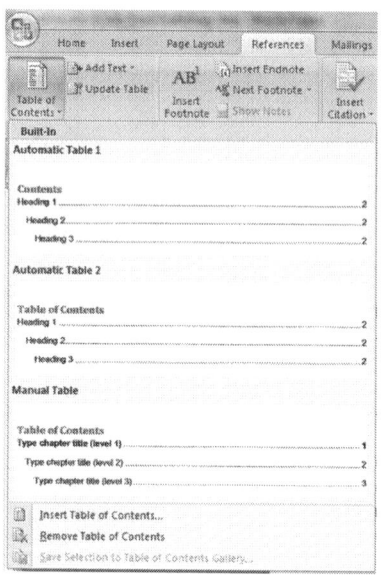

Select Table of Contents on the left of the menu and then select the Automatic Table 1. This will insert a table of contents for you.

We will be updating this later as we continue working on the book so don't worry if all your chapter headings aren't quite right at this point.

LAYOUT: REVIEWS

When you get the reviews back from your readers you should place some of them in your book near the front. Like your introduction these will appear in the free sample that people can download before deciding if they would like to purchase the book.

Take these reviews and put them on the page after the contents.

Show quote marks around the review and acknowledge the writer. It's up to you if you include a link to their website or include their business title, but these can be useful if you are trying to show your reader how the reviewer is qualified to comment on your book.

You can then consider using snippets of these on your back cover or in your book description.

LAYOUT: INTRODUCTION

This is the next page after the reviews page. It could be preceded by a Foreword if you have one though.

When your book is viewed as a sample on Amazon you don't want to give everything away, but a well written introduction at the front of the book will be an excellent incentive to persuade the reader to go ahead and buy the full copy of the book.

Your introduction isn't the same as your book description.

Your introduction isn't about you. You get your chance at the end of the book.

Your introduction only needs to be half a page long but should include the benefits to the reader, why should they read your book, what's in it for them? Try and include more than one benefit if possible.

Let them know what they will find in the book, for example, do you have an action for them to carry out at the end of each chapter, or a tip at the end of the chapter?

Make it welcoming, you want them to keep reading.

LAYOUT: CONTENT

This is where you put the 'guts' of your book, the main part of your manuscript.

LAYOUT: AUTHOR INFORMATION

You don't just need to write your book, you need to let your readers know about you and how they can contact you.

We will be putting these at the end of the book so our reader can contact us for more information once they have finished reading the book.

Your bio needs to be written to suit your audience. If it's a business book then this is your chance to showcase your business experience. If it's a fiction book then describe yourself and what you enjoy for your reader.

Where do you want your reader to go when they have read your book? Put a link to the website or blog where they can find out more information about you or your next book.

Give them the option to contact you for more information or with any questions.

Include a photo if possible, readers do want to know what you look like!

WRITE YOUR BOOK DESCRIPTION

Ideally you need to start this before you have finished writing your book as it's such an important part of the marketing of your book, and you will need to come back later and review it to ensure that you have it right.

This is the first thing that potential viewers see on Amazon and is your only chance aside from your book cover to hook the buyer and get their attention.

When you were looking for the book you were reviewing did you read the descriptions? A poor description can stop your book selling. Where possible include at the bottom of your description an independent review to help build credibility for the book before it starts to get its own reviews.

This isn't the same as the back cover 'blurb'. It's also not a rehash of your book content either. I have been told the ideal description is only 150 words, but I am not convinced. What I do know is this description has to hook your reader, tell them what your book will offer and make them want to buy.

BOOK COVER

I know you probably haven't finished writing or editing your book yet but it's never too early to think about having your cover designed. You need to give the designer enough time to complete the work after all.

Your cover will be the first thing that potential buyers see on Amazon, and the more professional it looks and the more attractive it is, the more chance you have of someone purchasing your book.

The quickest and cheapest way is to nip over to http://www.fiverr.com– for a measly $5 you can find many people looking to provide you with a book cover, but bear in mind they will probably charge double as you need a single file containing a front and back page, and there may be an extra cost for the artwork to be converted to the required Createspace format.

The problem with this is that a lot of them have all bought the same eBook cover graphics program, so you'll sooner or later find someone with a very similar eBook cover to you. That said, some of my favourite book covers have been sourced through Fiverr, it's a case of trial and error, and when you have found a good designer stick with them!

Your Book cover needs to show the title of the book, a strap line explaining what it is about, and the authors name. It may also need an explicit warning if your book contains adult content.

Your book cover needs to be striking and stand out. If you're planning a series of books, you need to bear this in mind, and find something that makes your set of books instantly recognisable.

In order to get the best from your designer you should ideally supply them with any artwork you wish them to use, and whether they supply it or you do, please ensure that it's 300dpi and even more importantly, you have the right to use it in print! Unlike a Kindle cover you will find you have to buy a higher resolution file if you're using a stock photography company and not all images are licensed for print use. It's your responsibility to ensure that any images used are appropriately licensed.

When I've used Fiverr I have always sent the designer the images I want to be incorporated, an idea of the layout I am looking for and the content I want on there.

In order for the cover to work you need to download a template file from Createspace. The template file varies based on the print size of the book and the number of pages. This means you need to know how many pages your book will contain at the relevant print size before you can start work on the cover. There is a small leeway of a few pages so even if you are waiting for a review back or want to tweak your content you can source this once your manuscript is completed.

You can download the various book cover templates from Createspace:

https://www.createspace.com/Help/Book/Artwork.do

You enter the book size (trim size) and the number of pages then click the 'Build Template' button. This will download a zip file for you to send to your designer. You need to ask for the artwork back in a PDF format and the file has to be below 40mb in size in order to be accepted by Createspace.

You don't need to know the ISBN at this point, just ask your designer to leave the white space in the template that is provided for the bar code as white space. Createspace will add the bar code when they print the book.

Here are couple of examples of the book covers that my clients and I have used:

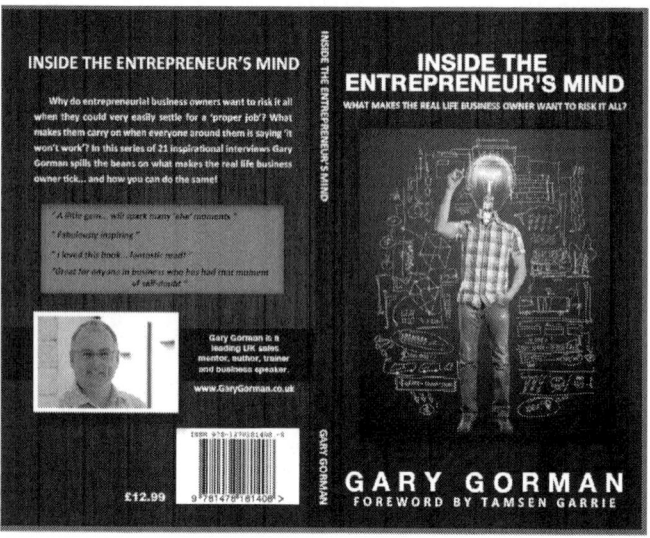

As you can see the single file contains the front cover, spine and back cover in one.

If you have less than 100 pages you probably won't be able to add any content to the spine, and even if it shows on your book cover file Createspace may well remove it during their manual review process.

If you incorrectly guess the number of pages and therefore use the wrong template the spine will not print correctly, it may bleed into the front or back cover. This is why it's important to know the complete page count before you get your designer to work on the file, but, on the same score, you can't complete your project without the book cover so do need to let your designer have the template as soon as is possible.

Unlike Kindle you now have to come up with the 'blurb' for your back cover as well. As with the book description, which we cover separately, this has to hook your reader and make them want to buy the book to find out more.

Don't worry about the ISBN bar code, the Createspace template contains a space for this and they will add this in at the print stage if your designer leaves the white space in.

PROOF READING

No matter how thorough you are, chances are you won't be able to spot all the errors in your book yourself. Where possible print your book content out and read it away from the screen. It's amazing how often when reading on a screen we miss errors that appear obvious in print. Another tip is to read it backwards, many proof readers have told me that this is when they spot the most mistakes.

As an avid reader myself I can assure you that there is nothing more frustrating than a badly proofed book full of spelling errors. It can really spoil the readers enjoyment of the book.

Make the most of friends and colleagues and get others to read your book and look for errors. If you're lucky enough to have readers reviewing your book they often feedback proof errors for you alongside their review, so you get double the reward from the review process.

The other advantage of getting someone else to read your book is that they can point out where things that appear extremely obvious to you just don't make sense to your reader. This is particularly relevant if you're writing a how to guide. You cannot assume that your reader has the same knowledge base that you have so you may need to explain some things in slightly more detail for them. Remember what we said earlier on about adding value to your reader.

It may be worth considering hiring someone for this task, just drop me a line at helen@hlsbs.co.uk if you need some help.

START THINKING ABOUT PRICING

You need to consider what is an appropriate price for a book in your chosen category. Do the research, see what other books in your genre are selling for.

If you price your book too low then you may find it is not taken as a credible offering within the category; if you price your book too high you may find you simply are too expensive compared to your competitors.

Createspace allows you to update the pricing on your book at any time once it has been published, but bear in mind it can show the book as out of stock for up to 48 hours while a price change becomes effective.

One of the major factors you have to think about in your pricing is the actual print cost. Even if you never order copies for yourself, you have a print cost every time someone buys your book from either Createspace or Amazon.

Your print cost is based on the size (trim) of your book, the number of pages and whether the interior is colour or black and white. I've only ever ordered books printed on white paper as I didn't like the one book I saw printed elsewhere on cream paper.

You can calculate the estimated print cost of your book and royalties using the Createspace calculator:

https://www.createspace.com/Products/Book/

Click on the 'Distribution and Royalties' option and scroll down until you get to the calculator.

Bear in mind that as Createspace are US based they show everything in $, don't worry, as long as you take the tick out of the box for 'suggest price based on the U.S. price' you can work in sterling or Euros as well.

First enter the size and style of the book you are creating:

Now enter your selected pricing.

If you don't know what to charge in $ then have a look at http://www.xe.com, it has a handy converter, you'll find this useful later when you're working out how much your own copies are going to cost you.

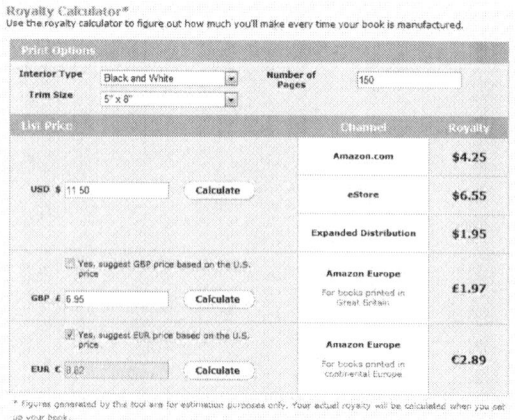

You can change the figures as often as you like, just remember to hit the calculate button to update the royalty element of the screen.

Using this tool you may find that your proposed selling price isn't high enough to generate a worthwhile royalty.

Before you jump ahead and increase the price try changing the font size to reduce the number of pages. Perhaps splitting the book into more than one book would help, remember what we said earlier about having beginner, intermediate and advanced all in one book?

Sometimes you just have to accept however, that in order to remain competitive you have to accept the lower royalty.

What's more attractive, sell only one copy of a book because it's too expensive, and make £5.00 royalty, or, sell 100 books with £1.00 royalty? I'll leave you to do the maths on that one. Let's just say apply common sense to your pricing.

If you're hoping to order books to sell via other outlets you will need to allow a margin for that retailer as well. The cost calculator will show you how much a copy of your book will cost you, remember to add shipping.

As an example (figures estimated):

Print cost:	£1.20
Shipping cost:	£1.20
Cost to You:	£2.40
Selling Price:	£6.95
Margin:	£4.55

Some retailers expect 60% off retail, this would leave you with pence, but... your book would be stocked in a shop. If this is the route you are going to take then put a lot of time into your pricing research.

DECIDE ON YOUR BOOKS CATEGORY

When customers browse Amazon they can select categories, in much the same way a library or bookshop would layout its book shelves.

This is an important aspect of marketing your book and ensuring that it appears in the front of the correct audience so you need to visit Amazon and visit the various categories available.

You may have some ideas on this from your earlier research, but you now need to finalise this decision.

If you want to find the right code for your category you can visit:

> http://editeur.dyndns.org/bic_categories

Remember, this is how potential customers will find your book so choose wisely.

SELECT YOUR BOOKS KEY WORDS

Earlier we looked at the category that your book will appear under in the Amazon store.

Now you need to choose the keywords for your book. Whilst this is optional it makes sense to give your book every possible opportunity in the marketplace.

These keywords are the words that can help your book appear in the Amazon search results.

Your keywords should be as descriptive as possible and are not restricted to single word answers.

For example, for this book we could select the following:

Print publishing, self publishing on Amazon, how to get your book in print

That has only used three of our keyword allocation. You could also include a keyword containing the word "books" - for example "Self Publishing Books" as this is a term commonly used in Amazon book searches to stop the search returning items from other departments such as electronics or music.

When selecting your keywords try and put yourself in your prospective customers shoes.

What phrase would they type into the search box on Amazon? Where possible include this phrase in your keyword list.

WRITE YOUR AMAZON AUTHOR BIOGRAPHY

You need to write a biography for your Amazon author page which we will create later on in the book.

You can make this different to your book biography which would have been more specific to the book. Your author biography should cater for the variety of books that you may write in the future.

Amazon require a minimum of 100 characters for this (approximately 20 words) and will only allow plain text. This means no italics, bold or html formatting.

Amazon suggest that you be creative, share anecdotes or interesting details about yourself.

If you are struggling why not visit Amazon and check out your favourite authors biographies for inspiration.

REVISE YOUR BOOK DESCRIPTION

By now you should have the first draft of your book description but now is a good time to go back and review it. You're almost ready to publish your book, and you now hopefully have some reviews or quotes to include in the book description as well.

Remember, that striking book cover and your stunning description are all potential buyers have to base their purchasing decision on if they are not familiar with your work.

You won't be able to get reviews from buyers on Amazon until after the book has been published.

Take another look at the description you have already written and add one or two reviews to the 'blurb'.

SET UP A LANDING PAGE FOR YOUR BOOK

You'll want to create a page on your website or blog that is dedicated to your book, you can start preparing this now, and can launch it the same day as the book is launched on Amazon.

Include your book cover image, your book description and anything else that you think will help your book sell.

Make sure you link to this page in your contact info page at the end of your book.

PROOF READ, PROOF READ AND DO IT AGAIN

Yes, I know you've already done this, but as this is such an important step I am going to ask you to do it again.

Chances are that you have made some edits to the book over the last few days or weeks, and this is your final chance to get it right.

As part of this final check go back to your table of contents and check that the page numbers are correct and all the chapters are listed there.

You can update just the page numbers or the whole table from within the references tab on Word.

If you are using word please make sure that once you have finished with the proof reading and editing that you go into the review tab on Word and accept all changes before you save.

SIGN UP FOR YOUR CREATESPACE PUBLISHING ACCOUNT

Finally we're going to set up our publishing account on Createspace (assuming you don't have one already!)

https://www.createspace.com/Signup.jsp?

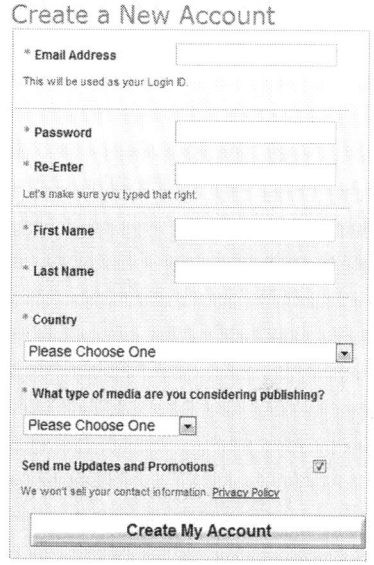

As you can see to create your account you need your email address (you'll need to click on a link in a verification email to proceed so choose one you can get easy access to), a password, your first name and last name (your real name if you're writing under a pen name), select your country from the dropdown box and then select books from the dropdown media box. You might as well tick the box for information as occasionally they send you a discount code for a free proof copy of your first book when you sign up.

You'll then be presented with their Member Agreement, when you've read it and agree with it click the radio button at the bottom of the screen to signify your agreement, and you'll be taken to the verification screen.

You can either click the link in the verification email you have been sent or enter the verification code manually on the screen. You will not be able to proceed until you have verified your account. This email occasionally takes a few minutes to come through so it's time to be patient, probably a good idea to go make yourself a coffee at this point!

Other information you will need to hand, and will have to be entered before you can complete your project, are your full address details and your IBAN and BIC codes for your bank account (these can often be found on your bank statement), although you can proceed without them for now it makes sense to do it as soon as possible.

Once you have verified your account and accepted the agreement Createspace will email you about the tax reporting side of things.

> *"Welcome to Createspace!*
>
> *Some things you should know about your account and how we report your earned royalties to the Internal Revenue Service:*
>
> *We are required to report your earned royalties to the Internal Revenue Service. If you currently reside in the United States, you must provide us with a Tax ID number, payee address and business type before your title can go live and be available for purchase.*
>
> *If you are currently living outside of the United States, you must provide us with your payee address and business type before your title can go live and be available for purchase."*

Now if you are a UK author you have a choice, you can either let Createspace automatically withhold 30% of your $ earnings and pay you the balance, or you can obtain a US tax identification number and have your royalties paid in full then declare them on your UK tax return.

There's a post advising you how to get a US tax number over on my blog:

http://www.hlspublishing.com/an-easier-way-for-uk-authors-to-get-a-us-tax-identification/

ENTER YOUR ROYALTY INFORMATION

From the My Account menu at the top of the screen select 'Royalty Payment Information'.

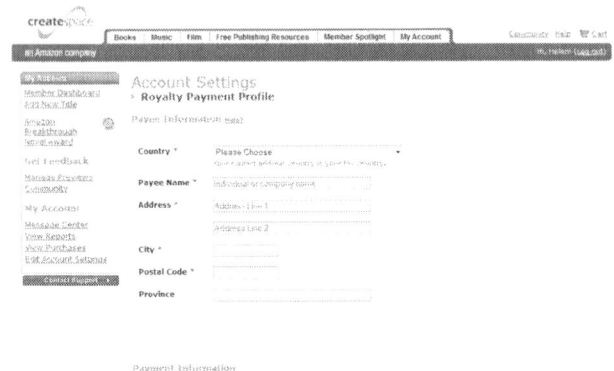

Complete your address details and payee name. Remember this is your real name, not your pen name. Complete all the fields marked with an asterisk.

Scroll down to Payment Information. I'm showing you how to set this up for a UK author who wishes to have royalty payments paid direct into a UK bank. It's a similar process for other authors.

Select direct deposit and EU using the radio buttons. Now enter the IBAN and SWIFT code (also known as a BIC code). The drop down box allows you to choose between checking and savings (current account or deposit account) and then complete the name on the bank account.

Scroll down to tax and business information.

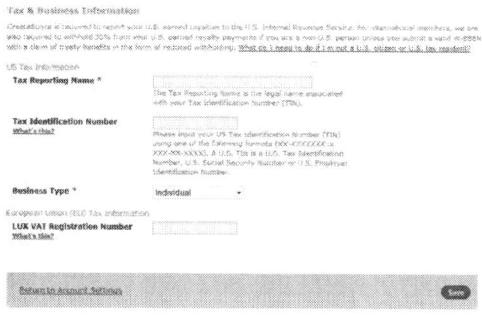

In tax reporting name enter your real name. If you have a US TIN enter it next or skip to the business type. If you have a VAT number enter it next.

Click on 'Save'

Createspace pay royalties, at the end of the month after they are earned, direct into your bank account, providing you have accrued either $10, £10 or 10 Euros. The foreign currency is converted into sterling when it hits your bank account. Each currency is paid out separately.

START YOUR FIRST PROJECT

Once you've verified your account you are given two options, 'Do it Yourself' or 'Call in the Pros'. I have never used the 'Call in the Pros' option so really can't offer any feedback on it, however, Createspace have a very active author community where you can ask other authors for their experience of the service. We're working on the assumption that as you've purchased this book you'd rather 'Do it Yourself'

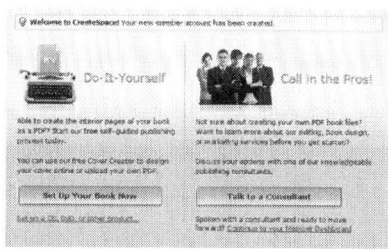

You need to select the 'Set Up Your Book Now' button.

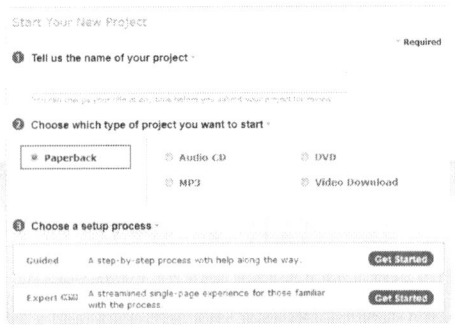

You need to give your project a name, if you've decided on your book title then you may as well use that. Paperback is already highlighted for you and next you get to choose guided or Expert.

I've been doing this for a while now and still prefer to use the guided process as it's easier to flick backwards and forwards if needed, and it's also the process I am going to show you over the next few pages.

SET UP: TITLE INFORMATION

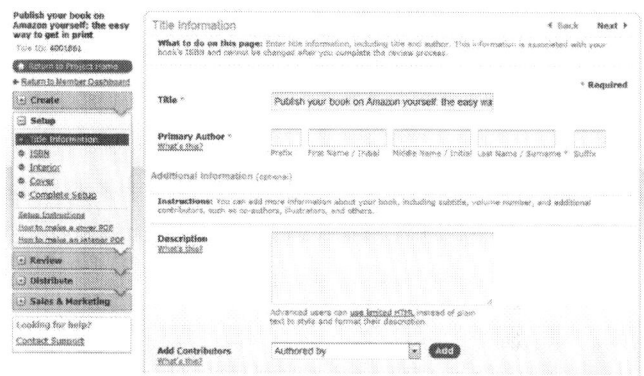

You're now on the Title Information part of the set up process.

Primary Author
Enter the name of the author as you wish it to appear on the book, this can be a pen name if you wish, but remember to put the names in the correct boxes. It's easy to type the surname in the middle name box if you're not paying attention.

Description
Remember what we said about your book description earlier? This is where you enter it, and the description from this box is the one that will appear alongside your book on Amazon.

Add Contributors

Have a co-author, or has someone written a foreword? You can add the additional contributors here. Take care though as sometimes these additional contributors transfer over to Amazon as authors, I tend to leave these blank now and add the information via my Amazon author page later if required.

Subtitle

If your book has a subtitle you can enter it here.

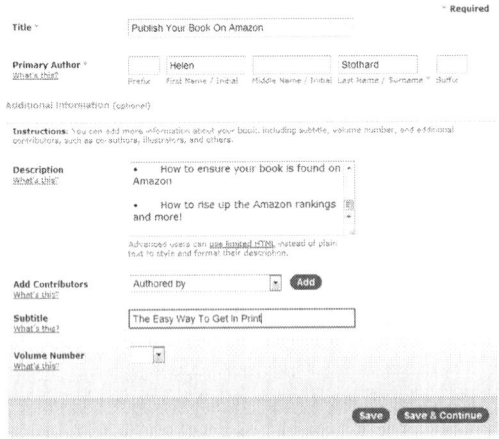

Double check your spelling here as it's often a screen authors forget to come back and review. "Save & Continue".

SET UP:
ISBN

You are now offered two options for your ISBN.

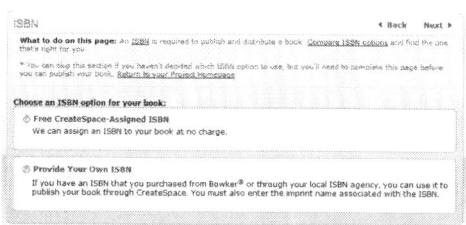

You can use a free Createspace assigned ISBN or you can supply your own.

To date I have always used the free Createspace assigned ISBN. It gets the book on Amazon, which is where I want to sell it mainly, and I can still order my own copies to sell at speaking events and the like. It also doesn't stop me getting my books listed on Waterstones website should I wish.

The only advantage I can see to your own ISBN is that firstly, you are listed on Amazon as the publisher rather than Createspace, and secondly, you can take your book files and have them printed elsewhere.

I have yet to find a cheaper printer than Createspace for the smaller quantities I wish to order. (You can order a single copy of your book should you wish, this is print on demand so you don't have to hold stock or commit to a large print run).

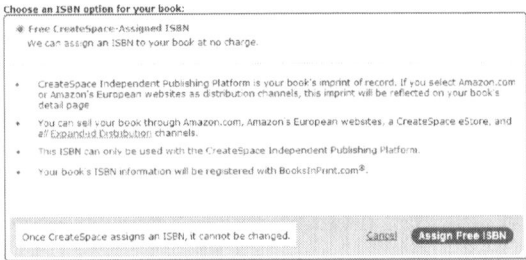

Once you have assigned an ISBN it cannot be amended. It should also be noted that if you wish to change the trim size, the interior colour or the book title that you will need to start a new project and assign a new ISBN.

Your ISBN is unique to this particular edition of your book and must not be shared with any other format such as Kindle.

Click 'Assign Free ISBN'. Once assigned your ISBN is locked and cannot be changed.

Make a note of the ISBN.

You need to go back to your manuscript now, and enter the ISBN on the copyright page. Remember to save your manuscript.

'Continue'.

CONVERT YOUR MANUSCRIPT TO PDF

I know that Createspace say they accept word documents but if you want the easiest and smoothest process then you need to convert your manuscript to a PDF.

Earlier in the book I stressed the importance of page size. Your PDF file has to be the same size as the proposed book trim size. Not all PDF printers do this, even if they say they do, I've spent many a frustrating hour trying to fix that problem!

The solution, you'll be pleased to know this is another free tool, is a download called DoPDF7. Once installed it acts just like any other printer on your computer. Simply select it as your printer and in properties ensure you have custom size to match the trim size and 300dpi as your resolution.

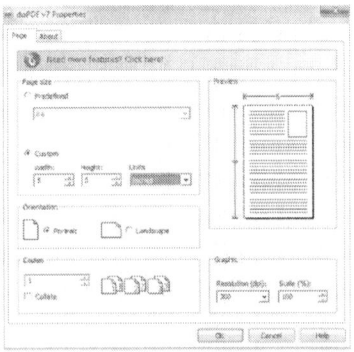

When you click okay it will suggest a default location for your project, you can change this if you want to make it easier to find later.

It's as simple as that!

You're probably sick of me going on about proof reading but you now need to proof the PDF document you just generated. So go ahead, roll your eyes at me and crack on with the proofing!

Do the pages line up correctly, do your page numbers match the contents if you have a table of contents, do the headers and footers appear in the correct place and style?

If the PDF is wrong then the printed book will be wrong.

If you're happy with your book interior then you're ready to move to the next stage in the process.

If you're not happy keep editing the manuscript and generating a new PDF until you are.

SET UP:
INTERIOR

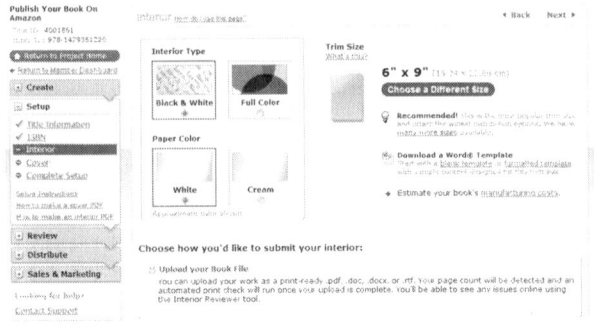

STOP! That's right, you're probably starting to get rather excited now, and that's fine, but the decisions we make on this page are fixed. Once we make them we're stuck with them so take a moment to look at what you're choosing.

Interior Type
This is where you choose between black and white and colour. Think back to what we said earlier, do your images really need to be in colour? Is it worth the extra you will have to charge your reader?

Paper Colour
White or cream? Every author I have worked with has gone with white, I prefer white, it just looks a higher quality to me when I view the book. It's your book though so the choice is yours.

Trim Size

By default the trim size is set at 6"x9". Click the choose a different size button if you want something else. Bear in mind if you select a different size to your manuscript you'll have to redo the manuscript and the book cover as well. Once selected it cannot be changed.

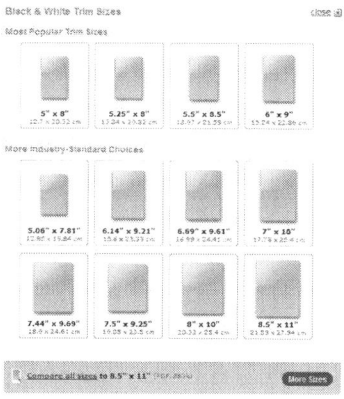

Simply click on the image of the trim size you wish to use. It will take you back to the previous screen.

Scroll down and you have the option to load your book file. Select the radio button next to 'Upload your book file' and it brings up the file selection box. Click on the 'choose file' button and browse your computer for the final PDF copy of your manuscript.

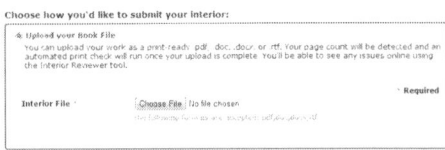

Once you have loaded the file you need to ensure that you have a tick in the 'Run automated print checks and view formatting issues online' check box.

I leave the bleed box at the default of 'ends before the edge of the page'.

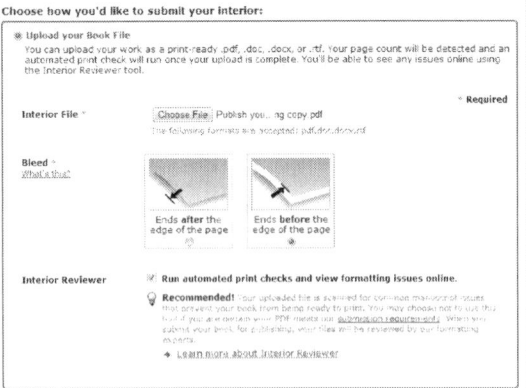

Scroll down to the bottom of the screen and click save. You now need to wait for the file to load.

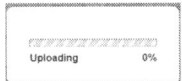

SET UP: AUTOMATED PRINT CHECK

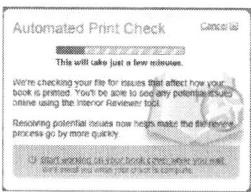

It's time to go get yourself another coffee as this stage can take a good few minutes. Createspace are reading your PDF file and seeing if their automated system can find any errors in the file. This is where you will find out if your images are too low a resolution, or your header and footer or margins are causing a bleed issue.

Hopefully when the next screen comes up it will have no errors, however, as this is a guide I've ensured my first draft does have errors so you can see how to fix them.

Even if there are no errors you should launch the Interior Reviewer, it's your final proof stage before you submit the book to Createspace for their manual review process. I know, more proofing, stop rolling your eyes at me and just get on with it!

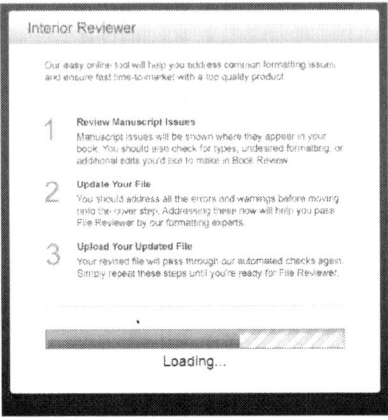

This stage takes a few minutes and then you have the option to 'Get Started'.

Let's take a moment to look at the review screen.

The top of the screen shows the book title, the trim size you selected, and the number of pages.

The centre of the screen contains your book interior.

The right of the screen shows any error information. Let's look at this first.

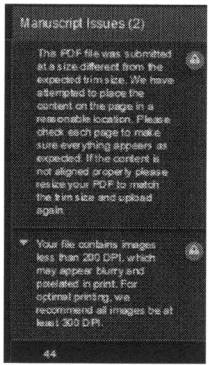

The first error is telling me that my file size is not the 5x8 format I had expected. I need to go back to my word document and check the size of the page layout.

I can reset this and reprint it to the 5x8 size again in DoPDF7 but before I reprint I need to look at the other error message relating to images.

By clicking on the little button to the left of the message it shows me the page numbers that are affected. Click on the page number and it opens your book interior to the image it is querying.

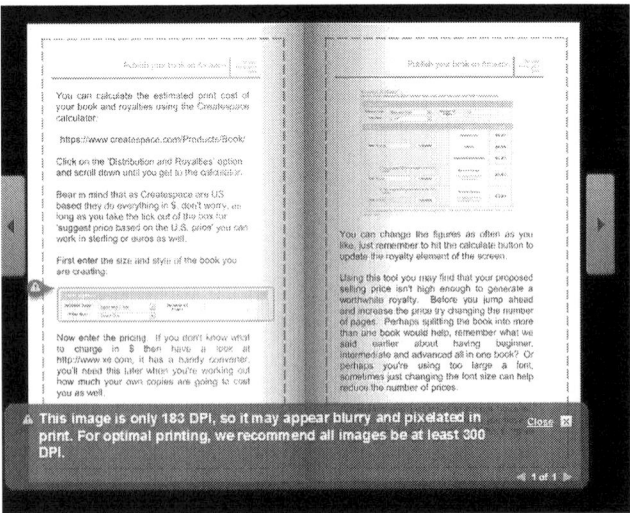

Okay, it's letting me know that the image is too low a resolution. I can correct this by finding the original image (remember how I advised storing them all together earlier), editing it again with Irfan view and then re-inserting it to the manuscript.

In the bottom right of the screen click on the red text 'Go Back and Make Changes'.

Re-load your amended interior file and start the review process again.

You need to click on the red text, bottom left of the print check message box to 'Upload a different file'.

When you have amended and re-loaded your interior you will hopefully see the following screen, if not, keep amending until you do.

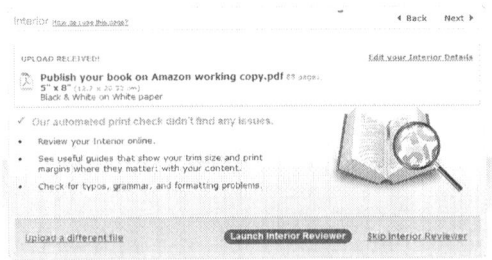

We still want to do this last proof of our interior file so launch the interior reviewer. This is where we are going to proof the detail.

If you look at the centre of the screen you can see the title page of your book. Click on the grey arrow to the right to view each page of your book, you can zoom in using the magnifying icons at the top right of the screen.

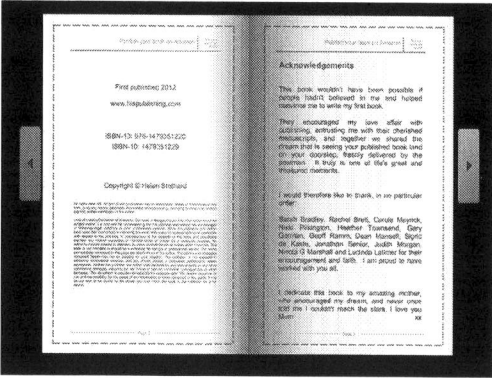

Before I proof the actual content of my interior I like to proof the layout. Are my pages lined up correctly? Are my headers and footers okay? Are my page numbers working properly? This first proof is literally checking the double page spread layout and making sure it works the way I envisioned.

Once I have done that then I proof the actual content. I know, you're sick of me going on about proofing but as it's your name on the book cover it's your reputation that's at stake here.

When you are happy with the interior click 'Save and Continue'. You're taken back to the review screen where you need to click Continue.

SET UP: COVER

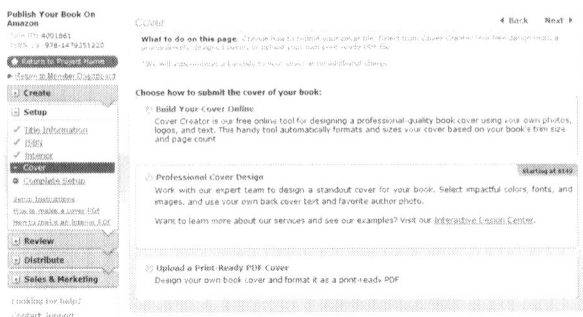

You have three options here but we're going to assume you wisely invested your $10 earlier or paid a designer to do your cover for you and go with the 'Upload a print ready PDF' option. Select the radio button and it will bring up the file selection window.

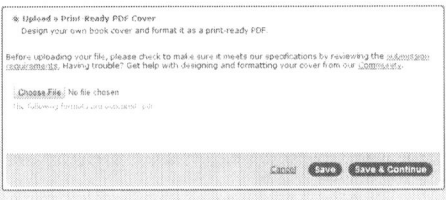

Once you have loaded your cover file select 'Save & Continue'. The file will now upload.

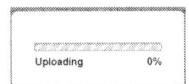

SET UP: COMPLETE SETUP

You're now ready for one of the most exciting stages of the project, submitting your files to Createspace for them to conduct a manual review.

Do one last double check of the information, make sure you have submitted the right cover file, then scroll down and select 'Submit Files for Review'.

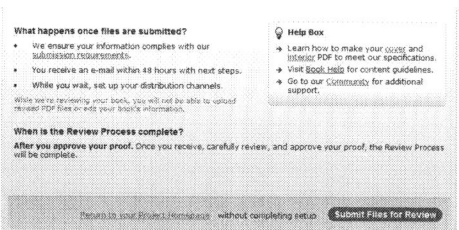

Createspace will now carry out their manual review process.

They advise it normally takes up to 48 hours but quite often I have found that files can be reviewed in less than 12 hours.

SET UP:
APPROVE
YOUR PROOF

Once your file has been reviewed you will receive an email to advise the process has been completed.

It normally looks something like this:

" *Congratulations your files are printable!*

We've reviewed the interior and cover files for xxxxxxxxx, #xxxxxx and they meet submission requirements.

The next step in the publishing process is to proof your book:"

You are then prompted to order a proof copy of your book, or approve a digital proof copy. The choice is yours.

If this is your first book then I strongly recommend that you order a physical proof.

This is the slower option but you need to see your book, feel it, and proof read it again! It has to be right.

Now I have published quite a few books I only order a physical proof from Createspace if I have used a different cover designer or a client has submitted artwork themselves. This is because I now have confidence in the work I produce and the systems that I use.

NOTE: If you order a physical proof copy the last page inside the book has the word proof in huge capital letters filling it. Once you have approved the proof subsequent books you order will have this as a blank white page.

You have the option to approve the digital proof and bypass waiting for a physical book to arrive. If you do take this option then I would always recommend ordering a copy first class from Amazon as soon as it appears on sale. Whilst this costs more it's a much speedier process. (Yes you've paid full retail but you'll earn your first royalty as well!)

Once you've approved your proof it tells you that it can take 5-7 days to appear on Amazon.com although from experience this is often the next day or within 48 hours.

Scroll down to the bottom of the screen and select 'Continue to Sales Channels'.

Publish your book on Amazon - the easy way to get in print

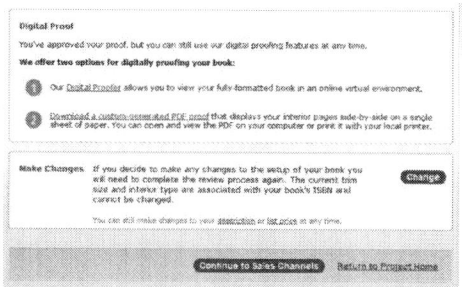

SET UP: SALES CHANNELS

Your book will be available on Amazon.com, Amazon Europe and also in the Createspace eStore. If they are not showing as selected then click to select them.

Expanded Distribution

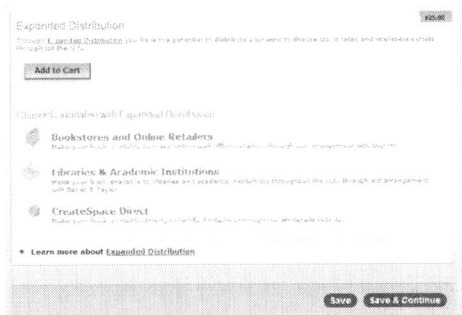

This is a cost option that allows expanded distribution through additional U.S channels. To date it is not one that either my UK authors or I have selected so I cannot comment on its effectiveness.

Once you have selected the sales channels you wish to use you can click on 'Save & Continue'. If you were thinking of only using one of the three free channels I'd suggest a re-think. You have done all this hard work so why limit yourself to the market places where your book can be found?

SET UP: PRICING

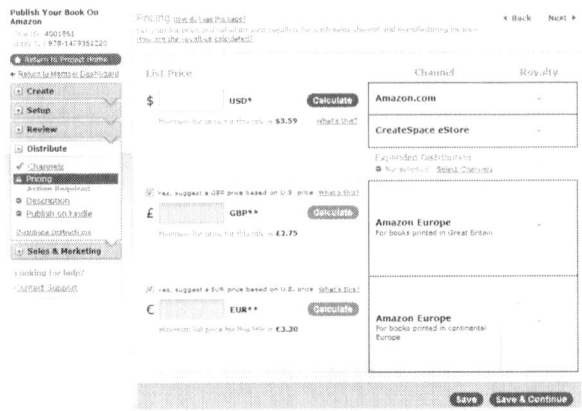

This is where you get to formally decide on your pricing, remember, you can amend it at a later date if you wish, however, it will show your book as out of stock whilst the price updates.

As we suggested earlier you can use www.xe.com to compare your UK price to your US$ if you are not basing them on each other.

It's better to set a price that fits your readers expectations of your book, rather than one based on your royalty expectations. The more realistic the price the more books you will sell, but also don't under price your book, that can hamper sales as well.

When you are happy with your pricing hit the 'Save & Continue' button at the bottom of the screen.

SET UP:
DESCRIPTION

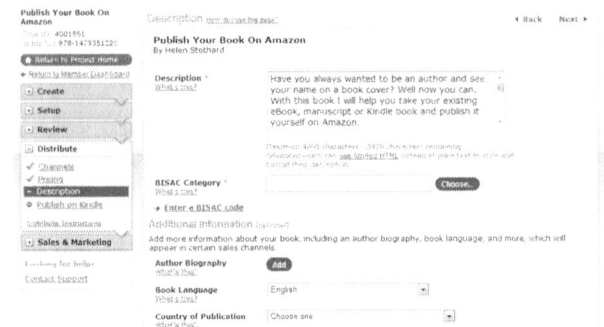

This is your chance to update your book description if you didn't complete it in full earlier in the set up process or if you want to make any changes.

You can either enter the BISAC code which you found earlier in the book or you can select a category from the drop down menu. Click on 'Choose this Category' to confirm your selection.

Scroll down and complete the additional information.

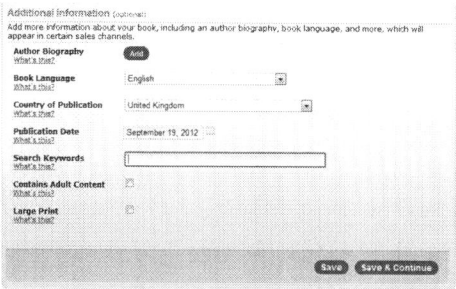

Select the book language, country of publication, publication date and enter the keywords that you selected earlier.

If your book contains Adult Content ensure you check the tick box.

Click 'Save & Continue'.

SET UP: ORDER YOUR BOOK

You can now order your own copies of your book from the member dashboard. Simply click on the 'Order Copies' link to the right of the book title.

Remember you can order one copy or as many as you want, but books ordered this way are printed in and despatched from the U.S. and are priced in $ as is the shipping cost.

There are three speeds of shipping, if you can afford it go for the priority one for your proof copy or if you must have books for a specific event.

Estimated shipping dates are given but these are estimates.

It should be noted that Createspace have a great customer service team who are quick to respond to any issues or customer enquiries.

YOUR BOOK IS LIVE

Once your book is showing as live in the Amazon store you need to get out there and promote it, writing it and publishing it were the easy bit!

- Place a link on your Facebook page

- Tweet a link on Twitter

- Put a link on LinkedIn and add it to your publications in your profile

- Blog about it

- Send a newsletter announcing the book to your mailing list

- Ask someone to do a review of your book and blog about it

- Ask anyone who has previewed your book to write a review on Amazon for you

- Update the dedicated book page on your website with a link to the book on Amazon

SIGN UP FOR YOUR AMAZON AUTHOR PAGE

Amazon doesn't share the author information between its sites so you will need to set up an author account for both .co.uk and .com markets. You cannot do this until you have a book published on Amazon.

To do this you will need:

- Author biography
- Author photograph
- Blog links
- Video (optional)
- Tour Dates for physical events (optional)

Amazon.com Author Central
Go to https://authorcentral.amazon.com/gp/join to sign up. This is the American site.

Sign in with your existing Amazon ID or create one.

In order to confirm your identity you need to select one of the books that you have had published on Amazon. Once you have found your book select 'This is my book'

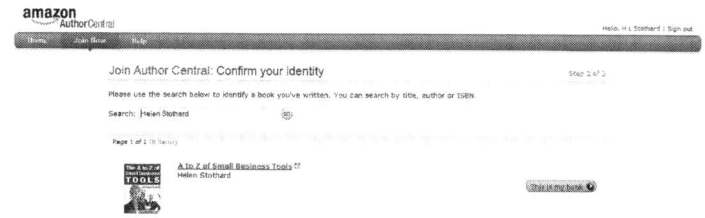

You can now visit your author profile page and complete the following information:

- Your Amazon author biography which we wrote earlier in the challenge

- Your blog RSS Feeds – you can add more than one blog

- Photo – add your photo

- Video – book trailers, interviews or book signing videos if required

- Twitter id – if you wish your last few tweets to be added to your profile

- Events – add any events that you will be appearing at, this only applies to physical venues

Amazon.com Author Central also allows you to create a url for your author page should you wish, which you can then share via Twitter or Facebook, or receive instruction on how to incorporate it into your email signature.

All the information you enter should update within 24 hours.

When you come back to your Amazon.com author page later you will be able to see customer reviews without having to search Amazon.com for your individual books.

Amazon.co.uk Author Central
The information you entered on Amazon.com Author Central is not shared with Amazon.co.uk so you need to set up a separate author page there.

http://authorcentral.amazon.co.uk/

You can sign in with your Amazon.co.uk id or create a new one.

As with the Amazon.com Author Central you select the books that you are the author of, then you enter the same information here that you entered on the .com site with the exception of the blog feeds.

REPORTING

Now we have our book on sale we need to know how to track our book sales and commission that is due to us.

It's as simple as logging into your Createspace account and viewing your Member dashboard. If it doesn't automatically open on this page then you can get to it via the My Account tab on the menu.

The top right of the screen shows your accrued Royalty Balance for the current month in each of the three currencies, USD, GBP and EUR. If you click on details in this box you can run various reports which show you different royalty information.

Further down you can see a list of all your projects.

This shows your book title, the book status, and the next column lists how many copies of the book you've sold this month.

AMENDING YOUR BOOK OR PRICE

To make updates to your book interior you need to amend your original word document and upload it again via the Createspace member dashboard.

Editing the book requires the same stages as publishing it in the first place. You can edit the book cover, if required, re-submit your book or 'save and continue' to get to the pricing page. You can also amend your book price here.

If you amend either the book interior or book cover you will have to go through the manual review process again, once you have passed this and accepted the proof your amendments should be live within 24 hours of being reviewed but will mean your book is shown as out of stock whilst the book is updated.

DON'T DO IT YOURSELF

Of course, it's all well and good knowing how to get your book in Print, but perhaps you just don't have the time or the inclination.

Well that's where I can step in and help you.

I have converted a number of books for clients into print format, as well as my own books.

If you're interested in having someone else do the hard work for you then check out my website which has details of our publishing offers.

http://www.hlspublishing.com

ABOUT HELEN STOTHARD

In 2009, I set up HLS Business Solutions to offer a virtual Executive Business Assistance service to coaches, trainers and consultants, writing my first book at the end of 2010.

In 2011 I started offering publishing services to authors and set up HLS Publishing Solutions in early 2012 to continue this.

I am known for my pragmatic outlook and Yorkshire spirit – and am regularly in demand for ideas and inspiration on how to improve administrative processes and implement social media within the business marketing mix.

I am a straight talking northern lass, mother to one, a business owner, coffee drinker, cat food provider, good friend, enthusiastic but slow runner and a twitter addict, not necessarily in that order.

I recently celebrated the third anniversary of making the jump from corporate life to running my own business and I love it.

Working from home allows me the time to be mum at the school gate and still get the buzz I need to be me (as well as pay the bills).

CONTACT HELEN STOTHARD

Helen Stothard
HLS Business Solutions

Tel: 01904 890212

Email:
helen@hlsbs.co.uk

Web:
http://www.hlspublishing.com

Skype:
hstothard

Twitter:
http://www.twitter.com/helenstothard

LinkedIn:
http://uk.linkedin.com/in/helenstothard

Facebook:
http://www.facebook.com/hlspublishing

Made in the USA
Charleston, SC
22 September 2012